TOP CHOICES FOR RESIDENCY AND VISAS IN BELIZE

ONE COUNTRY, MULTIPLE PATHWAYS

BY TASHA LAFAVE

WWW.MOVETOBELIZE.COM

CONTENTS

DISCLAIMER: THIS EBOOK IS FOR REFERENCE ONLY AND SHOULD NOT BE CONSIDERED LEGAL ADVICE. PLEASE CONSULT WITH PROFESSIONAL SERVICES WHERE APPLICABLE

ABOUT THE AUTHOR

Tasha LaFave

Hello, my name is Tasha LaFave, and I am originally from Peterborough, Ontario, Canada.

With a long-standing career in customer service, I bring a wealth of experience to my current role. I hold a college degree in Law & Security and obtained my Ontario Real Estate license shortly after graduation. Since 2005, I have been a dedicated Realtor.

In 2022, my family and I visited Belize and instantly felt a deep connection with both the people and the country. We decided to purchase a beautiful property and, by early 2023, relocated to Belize permanently.

Currently, I am working as a Realtor in Corozal, Belize. My aim is to assist you in making well-informed decisions about moving to Belize. Whether you are considering a permanent relocation, purchasing a vacation home, or investing in this stunning country, I am here to provide the guidance and information you need.

I encourage you to reach you if you have any questions, need guidance, or assistance with your Belize Real Estate needs. My email is Tasha@1stChoiceBelize.com

INTRODUCTION

YOU CAN TAKE CONTROL OF YOUR FUTURE TODAY AND CREATE A LIFE OF ABUNDANCE AND POSSIBILITY – BECAUSE WHEN YOU UNDERSTAND THE PROCESS, YOU CAN ACHIEVE YOUR DREAMS

Moving to Belize as a foreign national involves a clear and structured process designed to ensure a smooth transition to life in this beautiful country. The journey begins with determining the appropriate visa or residency option based on your goals—whether it's for retirement, work, or investment.

Key steps include obtaining the necessary visa or residency permit, which may involve meeting specific requirements such as proof of financial stability, health clearances, and background checks. Once approved, you can then proceed with securing accommodation, understanding local regulations, and integrating into Belizean society.

Navigating the process effectively requires careful planning and attention to detail, but with the right guidance, moving to Belize can be a rewarding experience, offering a vibrant lifestyle and a welcoming community.

CHAPTER I

BELIZE QUALIFIED RETIREMENT PROGRAM (QRP)

STREAMLINED PATH TO FOREIGN RESIDENCY
ADMINISTERED BY THE BELIZE TOURISM BOARD (BTB)

QRP Eligibility Criteria

The Qualified Retired Persons (QRP) Program in Belize is designed to attract retirees by offering a favorable residency option. To qualify for the QRP Program, applicants must meet the following criteria:

Age Requirement: Any person aged 40 years or older is eligible to apply.

Dependent Inclusion: Dependents can include the applicant's spouse and children under 18 years of age. Children over 18 but enrolled in a university can also be included.

Income Requirement: Applicants must demonstrate a minimum retirement income of US\$2,000 per month or US\$24,000 annually. This income can be from pensions, social security, investments, or other sources of retirement income.

This program is managed by the Belize Tourism Board (BTB) and offers a streamlined process for retirees seeking residency in Belize.

What Income Qualifies for the QRP Program?

As of 2023, to qualify for the Qualified Retired Persons (QRP) Program in Belize, applicants must demonstrate a steady retirement income. The income sources that are considered eligible include:

1. Pension: Regular payments received after retirement from an employer or government pension scheme.

2. Annuity: A fixed sum of money paid to someone each year, typically for the rest of their life, usually from an insurance company.

3. Social Security Benefits: Government-provided financial assistance for retirees.

4. Home Equity: Funds obtained through the equity of a home, such as from the sale of a property or a home equity loan.

5. Inheritance: Money or assets received from a will or estate.

6. Reverse Mortgage: Payments received from converting home equity into cash, often used by retirees to supplement their income.

7. Personal Savings: Funds that have been saved and set aside for retirement.

8. Retirement Contribution Plans: Income from 401(k), IRA, or other retirement savings plans.

9. Other Means of Retirement Income: Any additional sources of regular income that can be verified and deemed acceptable by the Belize Tourism Board (BTB).

To ensure eligibility, applicants must demonstrate that their total retirement income meets the minimum requirement of US$2,000 per month or US$24,000 annually. This income can be from a single source or a combination of the approved sources listed above. The BTB manages the QRP Program and reviews all income documentation to confirm eligibility.

CONDUCTING BUSINESS UNDER THE QRP PROGRAM

Qualified Retired Persons (QRP) in Belize now have the opportunity to engage in business activities under specific conditions. To be eligible to conduct business in Belize, interested QRP participants must adhere to the following requirements:

Application Process: Submit an application to the Belize Tourism Board (BTB) seeking permission to conduct business.

Business Plan and Investment: Provide a comprehensive business plan along with proof of investment capital amounting to at least one million Belize dollars (approximately US$500,000). This demonstrates commitment and financial capability to sustain the business.

Employment Requirement: The business must employ at least five Belizean citizens, thereby contributing to local employment and economic growth.

Residency Requirement: Show proof of having resided in Belize for at least 90 non-consecutive days. This requirement ensures that the applicant has a sufficient understanding of the local business environment and community.

Proof of Business Operation: Within 18 months of receiving approval, submit evidence to the BTB that the business is operational. This can include financial statements, employee records, and other relevant documentation.

CONDUCTING BUSINESS UNDER THE QRP PROGRAM

Additionally, under these conditions, dependents of QRP participants can also apply for permission to work in Belize, broadening the opportunities for the entire family to integrate into the local economy and community.

These new provisions allow QRP participants to actively contribute to Belize's economic development while enjoying the benefits of the retirement program. By following these steps, retirees can seamlessly transition from retirement to business ownership, leveraging their experience and investment to create a successful venture in Belize.

QRP INCENTIVES & BENEFITS

Qualified Retired Persons (QRPs) in Belize enjoy a range of attractive benefits designed to make their retirement more comfortable and financially advantageous. The program is aimed at encouraging retirees to settle in Belize by offering several incentives:

QRP Resident Card: QRPs receive a special resident card that allows multiple entries into Belize without the need for a visa. This benefit extends to both the retirees and their dependents, facilitating ease of travel in and out of the country.

Tax-Free Importation of Household Goods: QRPs can import personal and household items into Belize without paying import duties, making it easier and more affordable to set up their new homes.

Tax-Free Importation of a Vehicle: QRPs are allowed to import one vehicle into Belize tax-free, provided the vehicle is no older than five years from the current year. This helps retirees bring in a reliable mode of transportation without incurring extra costs.

Tax-Free Importation of a Boat and Light Aircraft: In addition to a vehicle, QRPs can also import a boat and a light aircraft without paying import duties. This is particularly beneficial for those who enjoy boating or flying as part of their leisure activities.

Real Estate Benefits: QRPs are entitled to purchase land for constructing a home or to buy a pre-existing home for residential use. This provides them with the flexibility to choose the living arrangement that best suits their retirement lifestyle.

QRP INCENTIVES & BENEFITS

Documents Required for the QRP

1. Submit Application Form (Request Form)

2. Notarized Birth Certificate Copy for each member of the family

3. Notarized Marriage Certificate Copy (if married and spouse is a dependent)

4. Police Record from last place of residence, issued less than a month prior to application

5. Notarized Color Copies of Complete Passport (including all blank pages) for each family member

6. Proof of Income, showing a monthly retirement income of a minimum of US$2,000.00 generated outside of Belize, in addition to 6 months of bank statements showing the retirement income deposits.

7. The written undertaking of deposit to a financial institution in Belize.

8. Medical Examination plus HIV test for each member of the family

9. Two front and two side passport photographs of each family member

CHAPTER II

MOVING TO BELIZE FOR NON-RETIREES

If you are planning a move to Belize but are not a retiree, what are your options?

You can enter, and stay, in Belize a couple of different ways. You can choose the route of Temporary Residence, Temporary Employment Permit, Tourist Visa. After 50 out of 52 weeks you can apply for Permanent Residence, and eventually Citizenship.

Belize Temporary Residence Program

The Belize Temporary Residence Program is tailored for business owners who have substantial investments in Belize, valued at BZ$500,000.00/US$250,000.00 or more.

Program Requirements:

Applicants must provide detailed evidence of their investments in Belize, which should not be less than BZ$500,000/US$250,000. The following documents are required:

- Proof of real estate ownership
- Bank statements (business or personal)
- Valid trade license
- Social security registration or card
- General sales tax returns
- Business tax returns
- Certification of investments

CHAPTER II

MOVING TO BELIZE FOR NON-RETIREES

**Belize Temporary Residence Program
Continued**

Fee Structure:

<u>For citizens of the USA and Canada:</u>
- Initial Fee: BZ$800.00
- Renewal Fee: BZ$800.00

<u>For citizens of the EU:</u>
- Initial Fee: BZ$1,200.00
- Renewal Fee: BZ$1,200.00

This program offers a pathway for eligible individuals to obtain temporary residence in Belize based on substantial business investments, ensuring compliance with the country's immigration regulations.

CHAPTER II

MOVING TO BELIZE FOR NON-RETIREES

Visitor Permit / Tourist Visa

Visitors to Belize can obtain a Tourist visa or Visitor Permit upon arrival, with the option to renew for US$100 per month.

Visa On Arrival Eligibility:
Citizens of the following countries are eligible for Visa On Arrival and do not need to apply in advance:

- CARICOM member countries
- USA
- Canada
- UK
- Australia
- New Zealand
- Mexico
- Norway
- Venezuela
- Costa Rica
- El Salvador
- Colombia
- Guatemala
- Brazil
- Japan

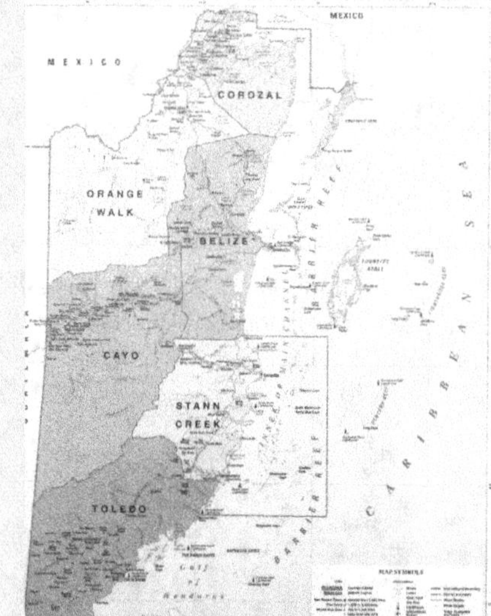

This streamlined process facilitates easy entry for travelers from these nations, allowing them to enjoy their stay in Belize without prior visa arrangements. The visitor permit renewal option provides flexibility for extended stays in the country.

CHAPTER II

MOVING TO BELIZE FOR NON-RETIREES

Temporary Employment Permit

Belize offers a pathway for foreign nationals to obtain temporary work permits, facilitating legal employment within the country. These permits are essential for individuals seeking to contribute their skills and expertise to Belizean industries on a short-term basis.

Eligibility Criteria:

1. Job Offer Requirement: Applicants must have a confirmed job offer from a Belizean employer. The job offer should specify the nature of the work, duration, and terms of employment.

2. Skills and Qualifications: Applicants must possess the skills, qualifications, and experience necessary to perform the job effectively. Employers may be required to demonstrate that no qualified Belizean nationals are available for the position.

3. Compliance with Immigration Laws: Both the employer and the applicant must comply with Belizean immigration laws and regulations governing foreign labor.

4. Health and Character Requirements: Applicants are typically required to undergo a medical examination and provide police clearance or a certificate of good conduct from their home country.

CHAPTER II

MOVING TO BELIZE FOR NON-RETIREES

Temporary Employment Permit

Application Process:

<u>Employer's Role:</u> The employer initiates the application process by submitting relevant documents to the Belizean Immigration Department. These documents typically include the job offer, proof of the company's registration and compliance with Belizean laws, and any necessary permits or licenses.

<u>Employee's Role:</u> The applicant (employee) completes their part of the application, which includes personal information, educational and professional qualifications, and supporting documents such as a valid passport and health clearance.

<u>Approval:</u> Once the application is submitted, the Immigration Department reviews the documents and may conduct interviews or additional checks as necessary. If approved, the applicant receives a temporary work permit allowing them to legally work in Belize for the specified duration.

Duration and Renewal:

Temporary work permits are usually granted for a specific period, typically up to one year. Renewal applications can be submitted if the employment is extended or if the applicant wishes to continue working in Belize under the same conditions.

CHAPTER II

MOVING TO BELIZE FOR NON-RETIREES

Temporary Employment Permit

Benefits:

<u>Legal Employment</u>: Provides foreign nationals with the opportunity to legally work in Belize.

<u>Contribution to Economy:</u> Facilitates the transfer of skills and expertise, contributing to Belize's economic development.

<u>Cultural Exchange:</u> Encourages cultural exchange and international cooperation in the workplace.

Obtaining a temporary work permit in Belize requires coordination between the employer and the applicant, ensuring compliance with immigration laws and promoting mutual benefit for both parties involved.

CHAPTER III

PERMANENT RESIDENCE

Benefits of Belize Permanent Residency

Becoming a permanent resident in Belize offers several significant advantages, making it an attractive option for individuals seeking to establish long-term roots in the country.

Key Benefits Include:

1. <u>Employment Freedom:</u> Permanent residents are allowed to work in Belize without the requirement for a separate work permit. This eliminates bureaucratic hurdles and streamlines the process for those wishing to contribute to the Belizean economy.

2. <u>Freedom of Movement</u>: Permanent residents enjoy unrestricted entry and exit privileges in Belize. This flexibility is particularly beneficial for those who travel frequently or have international connections.

3. <u>Pathway to Citizenship:</u> Permanent residency serves as a stepping stone towards acquiring Belizean nationality. After meeting residency requirements and demonstrating commitment to Belizean society, residents can apply for citizenship, thereby gaining full rights and privileges as Belizean citizens.

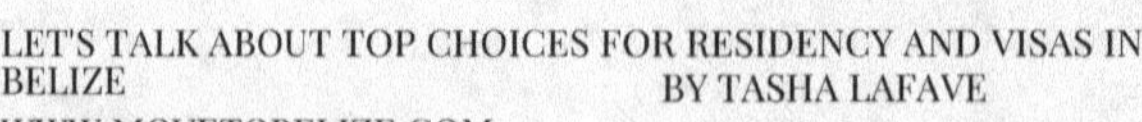

CHAPTER III

PERMANENT RESIDENCE

4. <u>Access to Services:</u> Permanent residents are entitled to access various services and benefits available to Belizean residents, such as healthcare, education, and social services.

5. <u>Security and Stability:</u> Holding permanent residency provides a sense of security and stability, allowing individuals and families to plan for the future with confidence in their legal status within Belize.

6. <u>Investment Opportunities:</u> Permanent residents may find it easier to invest in property or businesses in Belize, benefiting from local economic opportunities and contributing to community development.

By obtaining permanent residency in Belize, individuals not only gain practical advantages such as work and travel freedoms but also integrate more deeply into the vibrant cultural and social fabric of the country. This status represents a commitment to Belize and opens doors to a fulfilling life in Central America's jewel.

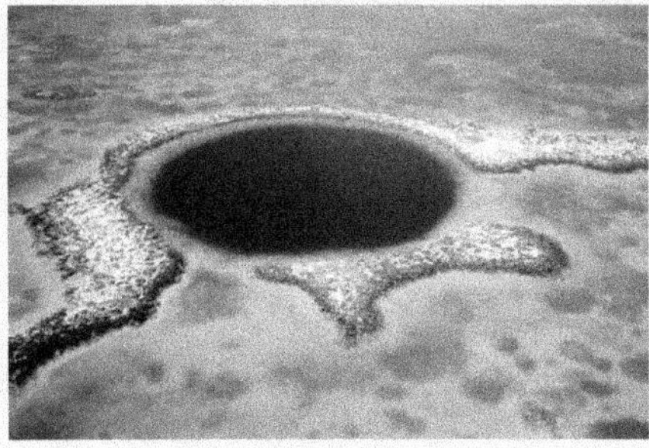

CHAPTER IV

CITIZENSHIP

Guide to Obtaining Citizenship in Belize

Belize offers citizenship to individuals who meet certain residency requirements and demonstrate a commitment to the country. Here's a step-by-step guide to help you understand the process:

1. <u>Eligibility Criteria:</u>

To qualify for Belizean citizenship, you must typically fulfill the following prerequisites:

Residency Requirement: You must have legally resided in Belize for a specified period, usually five years preceding your application for citizenship. This period can be reduced to three years if you are married to a Belizean citizen.

Good Character: Applicants must demonstrate good character and conduct. This includes providing police clearance certificates from your country of origin and any country where you have resided for a significant period.

Knowledge of Belize: You may be required to demonstrate knowledge of Belize's history, culture, and basic English language proficiency.

Financial Stability: Applicants should demonstrate financial stability and the ability to support themselves and their dependents.

CHAPTER IV

CITIZENSHIP

Guide to Obtaining Citizenship in Belize

2. Application Process:

Submit Application: Complete the citizenship application form, available from the Belize Immigration and Nationality Department. Include all required documentation, such as birth certificates, passport copies, proof of residency, police clearance certificates, and evidence of financial stability.

Interview and Assessment: After submitting your application, you may be called for an interview to assess your eligibility further. This interview may cover your reasons for seeking citizenship, ties to Belize, and understanding of Belizean society.

Approval: If your application is approved, you will be issued a Certificate of Citizenship. This certificate signifies that you are a citizen of Belize.

3. Benefits of Belizean Citizenship:

Passport: Holders of Belizean citizenship are eligible for a Belizean passport, which provides visa-free or visa-on-arrival access to many countries around the world, including the Caribbean, UK, EU countries, and others.

Political Rights: Citizens can vote in national elections and participate fully in the democratic process.

Employment Rights: Belizean citizens have the right to work in Belize without restrictions. They can also benefit from preferential treatment in certain employment opportunities.

CHAPTER IV

CITIZENSHIP

Guide to Obtaining Citizenship in Belize

Education and Healthcare: Citizens have access to public education and healthcare services provided by the government.

Property Ownership: Citizens can own property in Belize without restrictions, facilitating investment and residential opportunities.

Social Benefits: Citizenship fosters a sense of belonging and community integration, enabling participation in cultural and social activities.

4. <u>Dual Citizenship:</u>

Belize allows dual citizenship, meaning you can retain your original citizenship while also becoming a citizen of Belize. This provides flexibility for international travel and personal reasons.

5. <u>Continuing Obligations:</u>

Once granted citizenship, you are expected to uphold Belizean laws and responsibilities, including paying taxes and abiding by the constitution.

Obtaining citizenship in Belize is a significant step towards integration into Belizean society, offering numerous benefits and opportunities for those committed to contributing positively to the country's development and growth.

CONCLUSION

THIS IS THE BEGINNING OF SOMETHING GOOD.

Moving to Belize offers diverse residency and visa options tailored to different lifestyles and needs.

For retirees, the Qualified Retired Persons (QRP) program provides an attractive pathway, offering tax exemptions and other incentives to retirees who wish to settle and enjoy their golden years in Belize.

Non-retirees have options such as temporary residency permits, which allow individuals to live and work in Belize legally for specified periods. These permits are ideal for those seeking to invest, work, or study in the country, offering flexibility and a straightforward process to obtain legal status.

Whether you're retiring in Belize under the QRP program or exploring temporary residency for work or other purposes, Belize welcomes expatriates with a blend of natural beauty, vibrant culture, and a welcoming community. Each pathway offers unique benefits and opportunities to make Belize your new home.